The Heart of Worship

The Circumcised Heart
21-Day Devotional

The Heart of Worship

The Heart of Worship

The Circumcised Heart
21-Day Devotional

Latina Teele

Editorial Midwife Publishing

The Heart of Worship

Copyright ©2025 by Latina Teele
All rights reserved.

This book or any portion thereof may not be reproduced or used in any manner whatsoever without the express written permission of the publisher except for the use of brief quotations in a book review.

Scripture quotations are taken from the Holy Bible, King James Version, New King James Version, and New International Version.

Editor and Consultant: Dr. Lita P. Ward, the Editorial Midwife
LPW Editing & Consulting Services
lpwediting@gmail.com and www.lward.org

Cover Design: Bernadine Cox, BVS Consulting, LLC

Photo Credit: Jessika Patrick

ISBN – 13: 9798300021344

Table of Contents

Acknowledgment ix
Dedication x
Foreword xi
INTRODUCTION 1
DAY 1 3
   TRUE WORSHIP IS NOT JUST A SONG! 3
DAY 2 9
   WORSHIP IS THE LOVE OF THE FATHER EXPRESSED 9
DAY 3 15
   WORSHIP FROM THE HEART 15
DAY 4 19
   WHAT IS THE POSTURE OF YOUR HEART? 19
DAY 5 23
   WHAT IDENTIFIES A TRUE WORSHIPPER? 23
DAY 6 27
   I WILL GIVE YOU A NEW HEART… "THE SPIRITUAL SURGEON" 27
DAY 7 31
   THE GENTLE HEART SURGEON 31
DAY 8 35
   THE CONDITION OF THE HEART –PART 1 35
DAY 9 39
   THE CONDITION OF THE HEART – PART 2 39
DAY 10 43
   A CIRCUMCISED HEART – PART 1 43
DAY 11 49
   A CIRCUMCISED HEART – PART 2 49

DAY 12	53
THE BLOCKAGE	*53*
DAY 13	57
WORSHIP THAT MATTERS	*57*
DAY 14	61
THE HEART THAT MATTERS TO GOD	*61*
DAY 15	65
WHAT DOES WORSHIP MEAN TO YOU?	*65*
DAY 16	69
MAN'S HEART	*69*
DAY 17	73
A TRUE WORSHIPPER'S HEART	*73*
DAY 18	77
EXCERPT FROM "WORSHIP AT THE WELL"	*77*
DAY 19	81
THE NATURAL CIRCUMCISION	*81*
DAY 20	85
CIRCUMCISION OF THE HEART	*85*
DAY 21	89
THERE IS SO MUCH MORE!	*89*
KEYS TO BECOMING A WORSHIPPER	92
MY PRAYER FOR YOU!	109
"My Heart of Love and Worship"	110
About The Author	113

Acknowledgment

I would like to thank God for His Son, Jesus, who is my Lord and Savior! I can only do what I do in Jesus' mighty name. To God be the Glory! I thank my husband, Michael Teele, of 34 years, and our beautiful children, Michael A. Teele, Latilya Teele, Jeremiah Teele, and NyAriyon Santiago, our Mimi, our God-sent daughter. I do honor and thank God for my mother, Bettie Harrington, my Miracle Mom!

I want to thank Pastor Christopher Adukpo and wife, Sis. Elizabeth or Evangelist Adukpo of Temple Bryant-Mission Church of Ghana, Africa, and their prayer team. Thank you, Bishop Frederick and Hattie Hopkins, for the prayers and encouragement. I do honor and acknowledge my birthing place, House of Refuge Church Ministries of Robersonville, NC, Overseer Ronnie Staton, Pastor Angel Staton, and the church family. Many blessings to you all!

Breaking Free NC Ministries, thank you all for the prayers, love, and encouragement! Breaking Free 24/7 Life Line, thank you for every 5:00AM prayer for me and my family! Breaking Free Village Church of Ghana West Africa, thank you for the prayers. Better days are ahead, and God bless you. And to my book Editor, Dr. Lita Ward, thank you for always being there for me! Jesus be praised!

Dedication

I truly thank my Lord and Savior Jesus for this journal. I dedicate this devotional to my family: Michael, Lil Mike, Latilya, Jeremiah, and Mimi. I also dedicate this journal to my mother, Betty Harrington. I pray my family will take this 21-day devotional challenge. I'm a firm believer that ministry starts at home.

I thank God for giving me the strength to write this devotional, which will help many people see the power of worship. Worship is a life dedicated to God in fullness; therefore, I dedicate this Worship Devotional to God without reservation.

May this devotional be a blessing to every person who reads it and commits to the act and lifestyle of worship.

Foreword

I believe we are living in a generation in which God is looking for true worshippers whose hearts are circumcised. Prophetess Latina Teele did not merely worship well, but she might also write well. She worshipped because the need for true worship was her great concern.

From her *Twenty-One (21) Day Worship at the Well Conference*, held year by year, there arose teachings equaled by few women of worship in modern Christian history.

She writes transiently about worship because she is herself, transcendent in its practice. Prophetess Latina Teele is more than qualified to write on this subject because her entire life is an example of a true heart of worship invested in the truths presented in this book. We do not need more books on "The Heart of Worship" subtitled "The Circumcised Heart" that come from a theoretical perspective or that focus on outward mechanics. We need books written from hearts that are fully engaged and invested in a lifestyle of worship, and this book is one of such.

We need continuous growing revelation in the value of worship. This is God's weapon of choice to change the spiritual atmosphere in our worship places. Do not approach this book as just another book on worship. God wants to change your paradigms and priorities. Make an altar with

God, and receive a holy resolve to enter into an abandoned lifestyle called "Heart of Worship." This is a must-read book because it contains most of the things you need to know about a heart of worship. I therefore recommend this book for your reading.

Christopher Adukpo

Senior Pastor, Evangelist Temple

(Bryant Mission-Ghana),

Kasoa Akweley, West Africa

INTRODUCTION

Many believers today instantly think of a song when they think of worship. In reality, worship is more than a song. Worship is a lifestyle. It's really a matter of the heart. Worship is the posture of the heart. Matthews 15: 8-9 says, "These people honor me with their lips, but their hearts are far from me. They worship me in vain; their teachings are merely human rules. In this end-time Church, we predominantly see this.

This generation, we say millennials, has the assumption that worship is far from what Jesus stated in the Bible. Jesus didn't say just sing, but your song must be the worship. He said worship in Spirit and in truth; therefore, if the heart is not pure, it will be in your worship. The worship song is only the expression of your heart. Worship is the matter of your life and surrendering to God.

True worship costs you something. What does it cost? I am so glad you asked! Worship costs your whole heart. Remember the woman with the alabaster box? It cost her whole heart to enter the room and kneel down to worship Jesus. Worship is not worship from the lips but worship from a true heart. It's our love for God that draws us to live a life of worship. It's not lip service, but it's our service unto God.

Romans 12:1 says, "Present your bodies a living sacrifice holy and acceptable unto God, which is our reasonable service." Worship is a life surrendered to serve God with a whole heart, not your lips only. We may worship God with the fruit of our lips, but our hearts are what God wants to hear. Yes, He wants to hear your heart of worship.

Through the pages of this book, my prayer is that you gain a concise understanding that worship is not a song but worship is a matter of our heart. The song without a surrendered heart is not a worship song. No, it's just a song.

As you turn the pages of this book, I pray worship will overtake your life. I pray you will gain knowledge that our life is worship unto our Heavenly Father. Worship Him in the beauty of holiness. The next worship song you sing, analyze your heart. Check to see if your heart is in agreement with the song.

DAY 1

TRUE WORSHIP IS NOT JUST A SONG!

True worship is more than a song. It is a matter of the heart. If the heart is not in the right place with God, then your song is just an ordinary song. When we as believers sing in worship, God is not listening to the song. God is listening to your heart.

These people draw near to me with their mouths and honor me with their lips, but their hearts are far from me. In vain, they do worship me, teaching as doctrine the precepts of men (Matthew 15: 8-9). Clearly, this Scripture is teaching us that our worship should be the heartbeat of God. He stated clearly that the heart of man is far from Him. Sometimes, our worship is so far from God. We enter our services of worship, and they are so far from the presence of God. If our hearts are filled with resentment, unforgiveness, bitterness, pride, and simply our fleshly thoughts, there is no way that we will enter the presence of God.

Worship is our vehicle to usher us into the presence of God. Still, if this worship is not authentic, we're only wasting time with ordinary songs. God is listening to our hearts. A heart poured out into Him. Honoring God with our mouths and lips refers to the scenario here: "I'm about to sing this song, and to God be the glory. I honor You, Jesus; have Your way." God hears the vain words from the lips and mouth, but God is listening for the true heart of a worshipper! He said, "In vain do they worship Me. Honestly, you're not even thinking about Me. You want to be seen and heard by men. Because if you really want Me to hear you, then you would live a life surrendered unto Me!"

God sees the motives in our hearts. During our worship services, our hearts are so far from God, and how does God know? When our worship doesn't bring us in His presence. When we can call ourselves worshipping but can still hate, cheat, and live unholy lives. He said a life of sacrifice, holy and acceptable, which is our reasonable service unto Him. This plainly lets us know that worship is a lifestyle of holiness. *But as he which has called you is holy, so be holy in all manner of conversation. Because it is written, be ye holy; For I am holy* (1 Peter 1:15-17).

Holiness is still required for worshipping God. He is a Spirit, so worship God in Spirit and in truth. We cannot worship God out of our flesh; it will never work. This is why we see worship services corrupted with vain worship. This is why songs of worship are being performed by people whose hearts are far from Jesus; they are convinced by their own flesh that they can worship without a surrendered life unto holiness. How can one worship a holy God without a consecrated life? Holiness only means a life set apart for God, a life dedicated to God.

It is very sad because many people think that worship is our song. Do we really think that God only wants a song? This is God Almighty, the only true and wise God. The God who departed the Red Sea, rain manna from heaven. He breathed into the nostrils of man, and he became a living soul. Before Him, there was nothing. He is God, Elohim, Jehovah-Shalom, Jehovah Nissa, our Banner, Jehovah Raphe', our Healer, Jehovah-Jireh, our Provider! And all He wants is a song? Absolutely not!

God wants more than a song when it pertains to our worship. In our services, we sing one worship song, and we think that's our worship. That was only the expression of our hearts in the song. If we are singing a song with the lyrics, " I give my life as a living sacrifice to worship you, Jesus," well, if we are giving our lives to sin such as fornication, homosexuality, indulging in perverted activities, adultery, idolatry, stealing, and every sin under the sun, then singing those lyrics in the song, make us a liar. We haven't given ourselves as a living sacrifice to worship God. Romans 12:1 says to present our bodies as a living sacrifice holy and acceptable unto God, which is our reasonable service of worship! This clarifies that our worship is more than a song.

The Heart of Worship

Our worship is a life of holiness unto God; out of that life of holiness, we can express our worship through singing songs to God, but the song is not worship. When our hearts are surrendered unto God, our worship through a song becomes authentic. The ones receiving the worship songs in the service can sense or discern if the worshipper is just performing a worship song or if their heart is really expressing the words of the lyrics in the song.

I've been in service and discerned if the worship leader was worshipping from their heart or performing. This right here is significant to knowing the heart of a worship leader. The worship in the song by the worship leader takes you into the presence of God. This is an indicator that their worship is authentic. It's not the person only singing lyrics that are not part of their life. The lyrics they're worshipping are their lifestyle, and they're expressing it in the worship song. This is what we call true worship.

Romans 12:1, "Present our bodies," means to dedicate our bodies, set apart our bodies, and dedicate ourselves totally to God. The Amplified Bible says this is our national (logical, intellectual) act of worship. If the Scripture is telling us about how our worship is our life dedicated to Jesus, then we must live out this Word in our hearts. I will repeat it, worship is more than a song; it's a matter of our hearts.

The Heart of Worship

DAY 1 MEMORY SCRIPTURES AND NOTES

1 Peter 1:15-17 - *But as he which has called you is holy, so be holy in all manner of conversation. Because it is written, be ye holy; For I am holy.*

Romans 12:1 - *I beseech you therefore, brethren, by the mercies of God, that ye present your bodies a living sacrifice, holy, acceptable unto God, which is your reasonable service.*

_____

_____

_____

_____

_____

_____

_____

_____

The Heart of Worship

DAY 2

WORSHIP IS THE LOVE OF THE FATHER EXPRESSED

Worship is the love of the Father expressed. It is the feeling or expression of reverence and adoration for this divine status. Worship is the expressed reverence to God Almighty or a god. Love is a deep affection showing intimacy to someone. Our worship is love expressed towards God. God so loved the world; He gave His only son (John 3:16). This is a demonstration of worship of God's love for a lost world. God's heart towards us expresses His love and the rule of this love He sent Jesus. Expressions are the process of making known one's thoughts or feelings.

Worship is our expression of love to the Father. Romans 5:8 (ESV) says, "But God demonstrates his own love towards us, in that while we were still sinners, Christ died for us." The King James Version says, "God commended His love towards us." God endorsed us, yet while we were all messed up and still messed up. God proved He loved us, so He gave us His best. This is the greatest expression of worship. When we praise God, we're praising Him for all the great things He has done. When we worship God, we're

The Heart of Worship

worshipping Him because of who He is versus what He has done. We're worshipping Him because He's God.

Worship is demonstrating our love to the Father. Love is never one-sided; God loves us, so God demonstrates His love by giving His Son, Jesus. In return, we worship God by returning to Him a pure heart. It's the heart of worship that God desires. Let's use marriage for a husband who says he loves his wife, but he never demonstrates his love. How will the wife know that he loves her? Same as with our heavenly Father. If we never demonstrate our love toward God, how will He know that we love Him? This love has to be demonstrated. Demonstration is defined as a practical exhibition and explanation of how a machine skill or craft works or is performed. When we demonstrate our love to God, we're performing our hearts. We're explaining to God how much we love Him by demonstrating what is in our hearts. God had so much love that He had to perform it by giving His Son to the cross.

When Jesus hung on that cross, it was the most excellent demonstration of the love of worship. This is an indication of pure worship with no motives that are proven through our hearts. The heart must be pure to produce pure, authentic worship that opens the portals of heaven. There is no more significant demonstration of a pure heart of worship. Romans 5: 5 (NIV) says, "And hope does not put us to shame, because God's love has been poured out into our hearts through the Holy Spirit, who has been given to us." No love of our heavenly Father is shed in our hearts unless it is through the Spirit of God. Jesus said, "Nevertheless I tell you the truth; It is expedient for you that I go away: for if I go not away, the Comforter will not come unto you; but if I depart, I will send him unto you" (John 16:7). The Holy Spirit comforts us, and guides us into all truth.

The truth is authentic worship. Our worship can only be expressed and demonstrated through true love. That love is the love of our Father. Jesus expressed that love on the cross. To worship Him in genuine service, we can only express it in truth. How can we expect to worship a loving, true Father out of a heart that's not true to Him? It is a matter of the heart! A true heart of worship is what the Father is seeking. God has expressed His genuine love towards us; we must then return that same genuine love towards Him through authentic worship.

Here are questions we must ask ourselves: *How true are our hearts? Is our worship for real? Is our worship a demonstration of our love towards the Father? Is the expression of your worship, the worship that makes God smile? Is your worship the posture of a pure heart? What position is your heart in? Does it express your love for the*

Father? These are straightforward questions we have to ask ourselves so that we please the heart of our heavenly Father.

When we stand before God to worship, we should want Him to respond with His presence. *You will show me the path of life; In Your presence is fullness of joy; At Your right hand are pleasures forevermore.* (Psalm 16:11, NKJV)

DAY 2 MEMORY SCRIPTURES AND NOTES

Romans 5:8 - *But God commendeth his love toward us, in that, while we were yet sinners, Christ died for us.*

Romans 5:5 - *And hope maketh not ashamed; because the love of God is shed abroad in our hearts by the Holy Ghost which is given unto us.*

_____

_____

_____

_____

The Heart of Worship

The Heart of Worship

DAY 3

WORSHIP FROM THE HEART

This morning, let us search our hearts. Worship should be at the center of our hearts. When we begin to worship the Father, we must address what is in our hearts because whatever is in our hearts will come out in our worship.

This is why the heart has to go through the process of purification. We were born with a deceptive heart. If we continue with the heart we were born with, our worship will never be authentic. Genuine worship comes out of a genuine heart. This is a great example: Take a worship leader, give them the microphone, ask them to worship in a song and usher them into the presence of God. If the worship leader's heart is impure, corrupt, and bitter and harbors all types of sin within their heart, there is absolutely no way this person will usher us into God's presence. Again, it is a matter of the heart.

Jeremiah 17: 9-10 says, "The heart is deceitful above all things and desperately wicked. Who can know it? I, the Lord, search the heart; I try the reins, even to give every man according to his ways and according to the fruit of his doings." So, you see, the heart is not pure; it is deceitful above all things. It's not only wicked, but it is desperately wicked. How can authentic, genuine worship come from a desperately wicked heart? There's absolutely no way. God is holy and righteous; how do we expect to get the presence of God from a wicked heart?

Presence means "face," which is translated into Hebrew as *panim/paneh*. This translation denotes that the presence of God actually describes the face of God. Now, how are we going to encounter the face of God with a heart that does not have the character of God? We must examine our hearts, for God is seeking genuine worship.

Earlier, I asked how could a worship leader with a corrupt heart worship God. The Scripture John 4:24 explains how that would be impossible. *God is a Spirit: and they that worship him must worship him in Spirit and in truth.* We cannot expect to encounter the presence of God from a wicked heart. If our worship is not genuine, then it's vain worship. *These people honor me with their lips, but their heart is far from me* (Matthew 15:8).

This is the reason we're not experiencing the power of God in our services. The cause is what is in our hearts. Two songs by the praise team or choir will not get us in the presence of God if they are sung through corrupted, wicked hearts. Worship is more than a song; it is a matter of the heart. I believe we have really lost the honor and respect of our heavenly Father when we expect pure, authentic worship to flow out of a wicked heart. *Out of the heart flows the issues of life* (Proverbs 4:23).

So, whatever is in your heart is a demonstration of your worship. How can this be, you may ask? Your actions are an indication of what's in your heart. Demonstration is defined as showing how something is. If our hearts are not pure, it's going to show through our worship. It will demonstrate hatred, unforgiveness, bitterness, lust, and pride. This so-called worship coming from a heart like this will also demonstrate chaos and confusion. This worship will not be pure and holy, one that can open heaven. Pure worship from a pure heart is the worship that ushers the people into the Holy of Holies. It is the heart of worship that gets the Father's attention. He attends His ears when He hears authentic, genuine worship from a pure, clean heart. Our worship must extend from the heart of purification. Today, examine your heart and ask yourself, "Am I worshipping out of a purified heart? Is my worship genuinely from my heart?"

The Heart of Worship

DAY 3 MEMORY SCRIPTURES AND NOTES

Jeremiah 17:9 - *The heart is deceitful above all things and desperately wicked: who can know it?*

John 4:24 - *God is a Spirit: and they that worship him must worship him in Spirit and in truth.*

Proverb 4:23 - *Keep thy heart with all diligence; for out of it are the issues of life.*

DAY 4

WHAT IS THE POSTURE OF YOUR HEART?

The posture of your heart will depend on how pure your worship is. What is posture? It's the position of your heart. Positioning your heart as a verb refers to weighing your heart. As a noun, posture is defined as a particular way or approach to something. How does your heart approach God in worship? When it comes to worship, we cannot casually approach God. God is not casual. What is your perspective of God? It is a matter of our hearts when it comes to worship.

I am praying that the body of Christ gains the knowledge of the power of our worship. There is no power in our worship if it does not flow from a pure heart. This is why we do not see the supernatural glory revealed in our presence. God sees the posture of our hearts. It is a beautiful experience to worship God with a heart in the proper position or the correct posture. Psalm 29:2 says, "Give unto the Lord the glory due unto his name; Worship the Lord in the beauty of holiness."

How will we give God all the glory due unto Him? It is when we worship with a heart positioned towards God!

When we begin to worship from a heart of holiness, we're going to experience the supernatural power of God. We cannot continue to have a form of worship.

So many think we're worshipping God when we get one good song and sing it before the congregation. This is not worship if the song is not coming from a heart that is in the proper position. If the heart and the song are not directing the people to Jesus, then this is just a song for entertainment. Again, worship is more than a song. We will not encounter genuine worship if the worship leader's heart is not positioned towards God. Jesus called those who stood before the congregation with hearts, who were not in the proper position, hypocrites.

These people honor me with their lips, but their hearts are far from me (Matthew 15: 8). The heart here in this Scripture is not in the proper position to usher in the presence of God. This is a time like never before to position your heart. God is giving us time to get into position, the proper position, according to His words. It is a heart that is positioned to love like Jesus, a heart that's consecrated and set apart for the Father.

Our hearts are sometimes in the wrong condition. It's not consecrated; it's polluted with the things of this world. It is filled with the lust and pride of this world. This is the wrong position of the heart. However, we have a choice regarding the condition of our hearts. It can produce pure worship or vain worship. The Scripture says our hearts are far from God. We don't want to continue worshipping far from the presence of God.

We're living in perilous times like never before. This is a time to examine your heart. Make sure it's in the correct position to get the attention of God. He knows a heart that's in position with Him, a heart lined up in position. He wants a heart that's in sequence with the Spirit of God. He is looking for a heart that's lined up with the Word of God. Take today and get quiet before the Lord and ask Him to search your heart. I guarantee you that He will reveal to you the position and condition of your heart.

DAY 4 MEMORY SCRIPTURES AND NOTES

Matthew 15:8 - *These people draw nigh unto me with their mouth, and honored me with their lips, but their heart is far from me.*

Psalm 29:2 - *Give unto the Lord the glory due unto His name; Worship the Lord in the beauty of holiness.*

The Heart of Worship

DAY 5

WHAT IDENTIFIES A TRUE WORSHIPPER?

What identifies a true worshipper? It is the heart that is the identity of a true worshipper. Identity is the fact of being who or what a person is, or a thing is. Our hearts identify us as true worshippers. It has nothing to do with the outer appearance. This is how the enemy has deceived so many people in the past years. We fixed the outside up for worship, but the heart is corrupt. Man looks at the outside of the man, but God looks at the heart. The heart is not visible to man, but it is visible to God because our God has x-ray vision and can see through anything!

Jeremiah 17:9-10 says, "The heart is deceitful above all things and desperately wicked; Who can know it? I, the Lord, search the heart, I try the reins, even to give every man according to his way and according to the fruit of his doings." This Scripture lets us know that God searches the heart of man. God searches our hearts because our hearts are so desperately wicked. It also has a question and asks, "Who can know it?" Only God can see into man's heart. This is why God's glory will not come when He searches the worship leaders' hearts and discovers all these deceitful and wicked things in their hearts. God sees the heart that's not in the right posture to open up heaven, and when heaven is closed, God can't release the glory that He so much wants to release in the presence of His children.

God examines the heart, and sometimes, it makes Him regret that He ever made man. Now, that's very sad. Why? Because He created us to show forth His glory. A bitter, unforgiving heart full of malice will not glorify God. This signifies the wrong position of the heart. And who can know this heart? Only God almighty can know the very core of our hearts. He examines and searches the reins of our hearts because God knows it is desperately wicked and cannot genuinely worship Him.

We have to make a choice to examine our own hearts, purify them, and consecrate our hearts for worship. We cannot continue with this wicked heart. If we as the body of Christ, continue with this heart, we will see no true deliverance; we will witness no supernatural move of God. It's the pure heart that activates God and not our song.

I will, throughout this devotional, express that worship is more than a song. Worship is a matter of our hearts! Our cry in these last days should be, "God consecrate my heart!" If we want to truly please God, it's going to be through the purification and consecration of our heart's

The Heart of Worship

prior to entering His presence. A consecrated purified heart identifies a true worshipper. If we are not working towards this, then we are just sounding cymbals. Making a sound but not the sound of a true worshipper. Making a sound, but it's not the sound that opens heaven and gets the attention of God.

In this season, let God identify you. Let Him seek you out against the crowd. He is seeking true worshippers who will worship Him in Spirit and in truth. (John 4: 24) This identifies a true worshipper, a true heart. God is all truth, so why should we think we can worship Him outside of truth?

Jesus said in John 14:6, "I am the way, the truth, and the life; no one comes to the Father except through me." The heart is deceitful above all things; our hearts will deceive us to think we can actually worship Him, with hatred in our hearts at the same time. That will not work! Our hearts will deceive us into thinking we can live in fornication, homosexuality, and all sorts of sinful activities, and God would still respond to worship that attempts to flow from a deceitful heart. If the lifestyle is corrupted, then the worship will not be pure. We will attempt to worship but will only produce a foreign atmosphere to which God will not respond. God can identify the heart of a true worshipper, so don't think you are fooling God. Just be honest and allow Him to help you.

DAY 5 MEMORY SCRIPTURES AND NOTES

Jeremiah 17:9-10 - *The heart is deceitful alone all things, and desperately wicked; who can know it? I the Lord search the heart, I try the reins, even to give every man according to his ways, and according to the fruit of his doings.*

John 4:24 - *God is a Spirit: and they that worship him must worship him in Spirit and truth.*

DAY 6

I WILL GIVE YOU A NEW HEART
"THE SPIRITUAL SURGEON"

The previous day, we talked about the desperately wicked and deceitful heart. We saw in the Scripture that God describes man's heart as, in the worst case, it could possibly be. The heart only God knows, so this is the reason in Ezekiel 36: 26, God said, "A new heart also will I give you, and a new spirit will I put within you; And I will take away the stony heart out of your flesh and I will give you a heart of flesh."

God primarily promises to give us a new heart. This heart we were born with is not the heart God intended for us to operate in. The desperately wicked and deceitful above all heart is the heart of the world. When God gives us a new heart, He goes in and performs supernatural spiritual surgery on us. This spiritual surgery is like none other. God goes in-depth and takes all the hatred, wickedness, unforgiveness, racism, and deceitfulness out of our hearts. The key is we have the yield we have to yield to the surgeon. Yes, God is our spiritual surgeon; He has to go in like a heart surgeon and perform heart surgery on us to give us a new heart.

The only difference between God the surgeon and a natural or earthly surgeon is that God will not hurt you. God, the heart surgeon is gentle. God will go into our hearts and begin to strategically operate. He goes in and cuts all the blockage in our hearts, which blocks us from being all He called us to be. God will cut out that blockage of unforgiveness, which will cause us to miss blessings and fuel diseases. There may be some resentment and bitterness in the heart. While the surgeon is in there and sees it, God, the surgeon, will cut it out because He knows that it would interfere with the flow of His presence through worship. God is wise and all-knowing; He knows blockage of bitterness and resentment may seem as though it's a minor issue in the heart. Still, our surgeon discerned this minor issue in the heart has the potential to grow. It can't remain there because, in time, it will cause huge problems, such as preventing the flow of His glory released from a pure, healed heart.

God will cut out what needs to be out and all the bitterness, hurt, unforgiveness, strife, resentment, and all the other issues that flow from that deceitful heart. This great surgeon knows the Word is what this heart needs. As God begins to pour in His Word, it will help that person to do all that He needs them to do. "For the word of God is quick, and powerful, and sharper than any two-edged sword, piercing even to the dividing asunder of soul and spirit, and of the joints and marrow, and is a discerner of the thoughts and intents of the heart" (Hebrews 4:12).

This surgeon, who is God, knows the intent of what's in the heart, so His Word goes in and searches the heart while it's on the operating table. The thoughts that are in the mind are all in the heart because the mind and the heart are connected. This is why the mind has to be transformed; it affects the heart. "For as he thinks in his heart, so is he" (Proverbs 23:7, AMP). So, the heart must go through the spiritual operation by the hands of the spiritual surgeon. The Word of God is sharp, so it digs deep down in the soul and Spirit. In the process of cutting, it pierces deeply to divide the soul and the Spirit, giving us a new heart.

Today, relax and allow the spiritual surgeon, God Almighty, to operate on you. He knows what He is doing and has never lost a case!

The Heart of Worship

DAY 6 MEMORY SCRIPTURES AND NOTES

Ezekiel 36:26 - *A new heart also will I give you, and a new spirit will I put within you: and I will take away the stony heart out of your flesh, and I will give you a heart of flesh.*

Hebrews 4:12 - *For the Word of God is quick, and powerful, and sharper than any two-edged sword, piercing even to the dividing asunder of soul and Spirit and of the joints and marrow, and is discerner of the thoughts and intent of the heart.*

_____

_____

_____

_____

_____

_____

_____

_____

_____

_____

_____

DAY 7

THE GENTLE HEART SURGEON

The gentle surgeon is who God is. A surgeon is a medical doctor who performs surgery And removes or repairs a part of the body by operating on the patient. The surgeon is responsible for going in and correcting what's out of order. But when a heart surgeon is required, the surgeon examines the heart thoroughly.

Once the surgeon discovers the issue within the heart, he then schedules heart surgery. It is the heart surgeon who performs cardiovascular surgery, which is a surgical procedure that involves the heart and blood vessels that carry blood to and from the heart. Typically, if heart surgery is required, there is a blood vessel that's clogged. This is a significant issue in the heart that controls the pumping of blood through the vessels. Without proper functioning, the heart cannot function.

This is the same as in the Spirit. There could be an issue or issues that prevent the flow of love from within the heart. You want to love, but the bitterness in your heart is blocking the flow of God's love. And until God goes in gently

The Heart of Worship

and cuts out the bitterness and unforgiveness, His love cannot flow.

Some cardiovascular surgery isn't always necessary. Depending on the damage to the arteries, the surgeon may recommend some treatment to prevent a major heart attack. In the Spirit, God the ultimate's gentle surgeon may get to you just before major damage to your heart. He may see that your heart has some minor issues that need a little treatment, such as just some quiet time before Him or maybe a one-on-one conversation with the Father.

Allow Him to treat you with an outpouring of His love to heal that minor issue of your aching heart. God declared in Ezekiel 36:26, "A new heart also will I give you." The reason for the new heart is because we've been born with this heart of iniquity. As life goes on, this heart of ours absorbs all of the things in it that will defect our hearts, causing it many issues. Out of the heart flows many issues. Only the heart surgeon, who is God Almighty, can fix what is broken within our hearts. The only way we can be healed in our hearts is to draw near to God. James 4:8 says, "Draw near to God, and He will draw near to you."

So many issues of life overwhelm our hearts, which is why we need a heart surgeon. Only our spiritual heart surgeon, God, will go into all hearts and cut out the issues that are killing us. If these issues continue in our hearts, they will do precisely what they are designed to do; destroy us from reaching our highest potential. They will destroy us from becoming all that God has ordained us to be. *The Lord is near to all who call upon him, to all who call upon him in truth* (Psalm 145:18).

To get a new heart, we must call upon the Lord, admit we need help, and surrender to the heart surgeon. He also knows what matters in your heart. He has x-ray vision to try the reins of our hearts. He sees the heart filled with shame, manipulation, pride, lust, unforgiveness, fear, and every issue that's blocking the flow of the anointing in your life. The ultimate heart surgeon wants to begin this work on your heart, but you must call upon Him. Admit you need surgery and that you need it today. Lay on the table of surrendering, and let Him open you up and begin this supernatural surgery on your heart. A new heart He will give you. Let him cut out those stones blocking the flow!

DAY 7 MEMORY SCRIPTURES AND NOTES

Ezekiel 36:26 - *A new heart also will I give you, and a new spirit will I put within you: and I will take away the stony heart out of your flesh, and I will give you an heart of flesh.*

James 4:8 - *Draw nigh to God, and he will draw nigh to you. Cleanse your hands, ye sinners; and purify your hearts, ye double-minded.*

_____

_____

_____

_____

_____

_____

_____

_____

_____

_____

_____

_____

DAY 8

THE CONDITION OF THE HEART – PART 1

The condition of the heart is what God is concerned about. Sometimes, we can get caught up in so many things about our outer appearance that we neglect the condition of the heart. Condition is the state of something in regard to its shape or appearance. What shape is your heart in as a reference to its appearance in love, forgiveness, resentment, or pride? What does it say and appear to be? What's the appearance that you see? Examine it today.

Someone else can assume what's in our hearts based on the condition it appears to be. Sometimes, the appearance of the heart may not be the exact condition of the heart. This means that it appears to be full of love, yet in reality, the condition of the heart is loneliness or a foreign love. This confirms Jeremiah 17:9, "The heart is deceitful above all." It can appear to be full of love, but at the same time, its condition is corruption. This is how so many people are deceived by the heart of man. That person can look you in the eyes and say I love you. It could appear that their love is genuine, but sometime sooner or later, you will discover the true condition of their heart. This is when you will discover the deception that lies within the heart.

Today, will you examine the condition of your heart? God really wants inside your heart to ensure His genuine love abides there. True love doesn't hurt people. As we examine our hearts, ask if our intentions are genuine. This is important because our intentions will be revealed through our actions. *And God saw that the wickedness of man was great in the earth, and that every imagination of the thoughts of his heart was only evil continually* (Genesis 6: 5).

God repented that He had made man. It grieved God to see the condition of man's heart. God saw that man wasn't living the way He had planned because their hearts were wicked. The condition of their hearts was corrupt, so He rejected the idea that He had even created man. Now, that is something to think about. Our all-wise God wasn't pleased with the lifestyle of His people. We do not want to live a life so corrupt that the one who created you regrets He made you. This saddens my heart to think that God found no pleasure in His living beings, who should represent His glory.

God was looking at the condition of the heart of man who was made for Him, but they forsook His love and walked in with wicked, corrupted heart. It grieved Him because He didn't see His character, which represented His glory. To look down and see the land swarming in sin and His creation living a life of lustful sin was not God's plan. The condition of the heart was far from the heart of God. I can't imagine God looking for a person with His glory. He knew He had created us for so much more, but the condition of the heart had deceived man.

DAY 8 MEMORY SCRIPTURES AND NOTES

Genesis 6:1-3 - *When human beings began to increase in number on the earth and daughters were born to them, the sons of God saw that the daughters of humans were beautiful, and they married any of them they chose. Then the Lord said, "My Spirit will not contend with[a] humans forever, for they are mortal[b]; their days will be a hundred and twenty years."*

Jeremiah 17:9 - *The heart is deceitful above all things, and desperately wicked: who can know it?*

_____

_____

_____

The Heart of Worship

DAY 9

THE CONDITION OF THE HEART – PART 2

On the previous morning, we talked about the condition of our hearts. Condition is defined as "the state of something with regard to its appearance, quality, or working order." Let's look at Genesis 6: 5 (NKJV). "The Lord saw that the wickedness of man was great on the earth and that every intent of the thoughts of his heart was continually only evil.) The heart was continually evil, which means the heart always carried out evil deeds. That's hard to imagine, but it's true. That means that not some but every inclination of the thoughts of the human heart was in action. Inclination is a person's natural tendency or urge to act or feel in a particular way. So, whatever urge entered the heart, that person acted it out. They demonstrated the very feeling of the heart. If the heartfelt or had the urge to sin, such as kill, steal, lie, fornicate, hate, resent, or walk in homosexuality, that is precisely what the person did. Whatsoever the desire of that heart, the heart conveyed.

I cannot stress enough that our hearts must go through a purification process. Our cry should constantly be, "God, consecrate my heart!" Why should this be a continuous cry? Because the Scriptures say that every intent of the thoughts of his heart was continually evil. This is why God was sorry that He had even made man. It describes the intent of the thoughts of his heart, so it starts with the thoughts in man's mind.

As we guard over our hearts, we are guarding over our minds as well. Proverbs 23:7 says, "For as he thinketh in his heart, so is he: Eat and drink, saith he to thee; but his heart is not with thee." So, in the Word, it's saying that the mouth speaks differently than the mind speaks. Yes, the mind speaks as well. It speaks to the heart, and what's in the heart flows out in our actions. The mouth is saying something, but the actions are showing forth something contrary. It's called a seriously troubled heart condition.

Constantly monitor a person's actions, not what they say. It's the actions because the heart speaks loud through our actions. If a person says they love you, then the actions must be aligned with the speaking of their words. This is why God said, "If you love me, you will keep my commandments." The actions from those words, "I love you," are keeping God's commandments because love is an action word!

This is why in Genesis 6:5, God regretted he had made man; the wickedness of man's heart did not show forth the love for their actions. Their actions reveal that they didn't love God. It grieved God because He didn't create man to walk in wickedness and malice. God is love and only love.

The demonstration of that love is Jesus. This is the reason He came. God gave His only begotten son to redeem us. Our hearts were not showing forth the love of the Father. The condition was not love, patience, joy, peace, long-suffering, faith, meekness, compassion, the fruit of the Spirit in Galatians 5: 22-23. These are the characteristics of God, and they were not conditioned in man's heart. The condition of the heart was jealousy, striving, envy, selfishness, and wickedness. Our heart condition grieved the Father in such a way that He was pained and regretted that He ever made man.

That's something to really think about. We don't want to live in such a way it grieves God. Yes, God has feelings too. He hurts, too, because even Jesus said He's touched by the feeling of our infirmities. Examine the condition of your heart today. Be willing to make a change of heart. Make God smile, not grieve that He made us. What is the condition of your heart?

DAY 9 MEMORY SCRIPTURES AND NOTES

Genesis 6:5 (KJV) - *And GOD saw that the wickedness of man was great in the earth, and that every imagination of the thoughts of his heart was only evil continually.*

Proverbs 23:7 – *For as he thinketh in his heart, so is he.*

DAY 10

A CIRCUMCISED HEART – PART 1

Circumcision is the cutting away of the foreskin of male genitalia. The word *circumcision* derives from the Latin *circum* (meaning 'around') and *caedere* (meaning 'to cut'). (Anwar MS, Munawar F, Anwar Q. Circumcision: a religious obligation or 'the cruellest of cuts'? Br J Gen Pract. 2010 Jan;60(570):59-61. doi: 10.3399/bjgp10X482194. PMID: 20040177; PMCID: PMC2801794.)

In the Bible, circumcision was established as a covenant between man and God that every male child shall be circumcised. This was an outward physical sign of the eternal covenant between God and the Jewish people. "This is My covenant which you shall keep, between Me and you and your descendants after you: Every male child among you shall be circumcised; and you shall be circumcised in the flesh of your foreskins, and it shall be a sign of the covenant between Me and you" (Genesis 17:10-11, NKJV). This Scripture refers to the natural circumcision of the male, but I want to talk to you about the circumcision of the heart.

There are some things in our hearts that have to be cut away. Yes, there must be a cutting away from all the corruption in our hearts that only blocks our blessing. Since there is a blockage in our hearts, we need to identify it and surrender to the Spiritual Surgeon, God Almighty, to operate on our hearts. Lord, circumcise my heart!

I want to bring your attention to Romans 2:17-29. Verse 17-18 says, "Indeed you are called a Jew, and rest on the law, and make your boast in God, you know his will and approved the things that are most excellent because you are instructed by the law." Here, Paul was criticizing the ones claiming to obey the law. You are confident in the Word because you know it, but are you living it? You are confident that you're a guide to the blind and a light to those in darkness. But in verses 21-25, Paul asks a question... You who preach that a man should not steal, do you steal? You who say, "Do not commit adultery," do you commit adultery? You who abhor idols, do you rob temples? You who make your boast in the law, do you dishonor God through breaking the law? As it is written, the name of God is blasphemed among the Gentiles because of you.

Circumcision indeed has its merit if you keep the law, but if you are a breaker of the law, your circumcision becomes uncircumcision. Paul was saying circumcision was a sign of the covenant of Abraham, but only if it was kept. But if God's law was broken, then their circumcision was useless. God needs us to have a circumcision without hands. Paul asks some questions in verses twenty-one and twenty-

The Heart of Worship

two. You know how to preach to others because you're familiar with the Scriptures, but what about your heart?

Even today, many leaders stand behind the pulpit preaching against all these sins, but if God were to put our hearts on x-ray, what would He see? What will people see? Paul called out the ones hiding behind their religious covenants. Today, we cannot hide behind our titles, our denominations, and legalistic values. The Jews had confidence in their own works; they became complacent in their own selfish ways. Teaching others about how they needed circumcision, and yet they were not circumcised in their hearts. The circumcision with hands benefited them nothing. It was the circumcision of the heart God was looking for.

Acts 7:51 says, "You stiff-necked and uncircumcised in heart and ears! You always resist the Holy Spirit; as your fathers did, so do you." He said to be circumcised so we will be no more stiff-necked rebellious people. They were rebellious, hearing only what they wanted to hear. Uncircumcised hearts and ears refuse righteousness. Don't let this be you!

The Heart of Worship

DAY 10 MEMORY SCRIPTURES AND NOTES

Romans 2:17-29 - Indeed you are called a Jew, and rest on the law, and make your boast in God, and know His will, and approve the things that are excellent, being instructed out of the law, and are confident that you yourself are a guide to the blind, a light to those who are in darkness, an instructor of the foolish, a teacher of babes, having the form of knowledge and truth in the law. You, therefore, who teach another, do you not teach yourself? You who preach that a man should not steal, do you steal? You who say, "Do not commit adultery," do you commit adultery? You who abhor idols, do you rob temples? You who make your boast in the law, do you dishonor God through breaking the law? For "the name of God is blasphemed among the Gentiles because of you," as it is written. For circumcision is indeed profitable if you keep the law; but if you are a breaker of the law, your circumcision has become uncircumcision. Therefore, if an uncircumcised man keeps the righteous requirements of the law, will not his uncircumcision be counted as circumcision? And will not the physically uncircumcised, if he fulfills the law, judge you who, even with your written code and circumcision, are a transgressor of the law? For he is not a Jew who is one outwardly, nor is circumcision that which is outward in the flesh; but he is a Jew who is one inwardly; and circumcision is that of the heart, in the Spirit, not in the letter; whose praise is not from men but from God.

Genesis 17:10 - *This is my covenant, which you shall keep, between me and you and your offspring after you: Every male among you shall be circumcised.*

Acts 7:51-52 - *You stiff-necked and uncircumcised in heart and ears! You always resist the Holy Spirit; as your fathers did, so do you. Which of the prophets did your fathers not persecute? And they killed those who foretold the coming of the Just One, of whom you now have become the betrayers and murderers,*

The Heart of Worship

The Heart of Worship

DAY 11

A CIRCUMCISED HEART – PART 2

Our worship must extend from a circumcised heart. In these last few months of talking about circumcision of the heart, I noticed it seems uncomfortable and painful for many people to listen to this instruction. Circumcision is painful because, even in the natural, it's a cutting away. In the Spirit, we don't want something to be cut out of our lives. So, it is natural; it's the same in the Spirit. Sometimes, God says, "Cut yourself from that person or that group of people." He may be pulling you up to another level. Still, He cannot because you refuse to cut the contaminants and toxic relationships from your life.

Your worship may not be pure because your heart is not circumcised. You refuse to cut those things away. We hold tight to toxic things in our hearts. What affects our hearts affects our worship. It's through a pure heart surrendered to the Father, living a life of righteousness that produces pure worship. This circumcision is working through the Spirit of God, not the circumcision of hands.

"Look: I, Paul, say to you that if you accept circumcision, Christ will be of no advantage to you. I testify again to every man who accepts circumcision that he is obligated to keep the whole law. You are severed from Christ, you who would be justified by the law; you have fallen away from grace. For through the Spirit, by faith, we eagerly wait for the hope of righteousness. For in Christ Jesus, neither circumcision nor uncircumcision counts for anything, but only faith working through love" (Galatians 5:2-6). Paul noted that it was great because you became circumcised through the religious requirement and the covenant God made with Abraham. However, it doesn't profit you anything if you're not circumcised through the Spirit.

Our work will never save us. Our works will never replace the works in the Spirit. No ritual, no religious act will ever replace or justify having a heart circumcised unto God so that we can freely worship God in Spirit and in truth. The religious people thought that if they were circumcised naturally, they could live unrighteously, and it was justified through their religious or covenant agreement to be circumcised. Whether you're circumcised or uncircumcised depends on how pure your worship is. Worship from a circumcised heart brings in the glory of God.

This is what legalistic religion does. It causes people to think that if they keep their daily, weekly, or annual religious rituals, it will justify them to be saved and holy.

Some do a Holy Communion each year, ask God to forgive them of their sins, and then after the Holy Communion, they go back to their wicked ways. They continue with an uncircumcised heart as if God cannot see the heart. Man cannot, but your actions can and will reveal a wicked heart. When you display fake actions before our Christian friends or our church members, they still may not see your foreign, uncircumcised heart. *Thus says the Lord God: "No foreigner, uncircumcised in heart or uncircumcised in flesh, shall enter My sanctuary, including any foreigner who is among the children of Israel* (Ezekiel 44:9 (NKJV)).

Nevertheless, God can see it because He has X-ray vision. He searches the realms of our hearts to repay every man according to the fruits of his doings. So, if your heart is uncircumcised, our heavenly Father sees it.

Circumcision is painful; it's painful to all your flesh, but if we do not, we will continue to fulfill the lust of our flesh. There is a glory God is ready to release, but He's only releasing it upon a circumcised heart. We must endure the pain of cutting toxic relationships off of us. Endure the pain of cutting off substances that we know are toxic to the heart. Circumcise the heart fully so you can give God the true worship that He deserves. We want God to receive our worship and He only responds to worship that comes from a circumcised heart.

The Heart of Worship

DAY 11 MEMORY SCRIPTURES AND NOTES

Galatians 5:2-6 - *Indeed I, Paul, say to you that if you become circumcised, Christ will profit you nothing. And I testify again to every man who becomes circumcised that he is a debtor to keep the whole law. You have become estranged from Christ, you who attempt to be justified by law; you have fallen from grace. For we through the Spirit eagerly wait for the hope of righteousness by faith. For in Christ Jesus neither circumcision nor uncircumcision avails anything, but faith working through love.*

Romans 2:25-27 - *For circumcision is indeed profitable if you keep the law; but if you are a breaker of the law, your circumcision has become uncircumcision. Therefore, if an uncircumcised man keeps the righteous requirements of the law, will not his uncircumcision be counted as circumcision? And will not the physically uncircumcised, if he fulfills the law, judge you who, even with your written code and circumcision, are a transgressor of the law?*

_____

_____

_____

_____

_____

_____

_____

_____

DAY 12
THE BLOCKAGE

What's blocking your true worship? What is in your heart that's hindering the flow of worship and God's supernatural glory? God is grieved as He was in Genesis 6: 5-6. The Lord was sorry He had made man on the earth and was grieved. I genuinely believe what grieved God was that they weren't doing what He had created them to do, and that was to worship Him. Sorrowfully, man today is still grieving the heart of God. Man's heart is wicked and more wicked than the days of Noah. So again, what's blocking your heart? What is in your heart that displeases God in such a way that He refuses to receive your worship?

In a person's natural heart, if there is a blockage that hinders the flow of blood transfer through arteries, the heart cannot beat. When someone has a heart attack, it's because there is a blockage preventing the flow of blood from pumping to the heart. I'm giving a simple, straightforward illustration because God created me to be a simplistic writer, and I am okay with that. As long as you understand that if you have anything in your heart that is not of God, this is a blockage. If you have unforgiveness in your heart, this is a

The Heart of Worship

blockage. If you have jealousy and strife in your heart, this is a blockage. This blockage prevents the flow of pure worship from your heart. Again, identify what your blockage is.

They may have rejected you, betrayed you, or scandalized your name when all you tried to do was help them. Let it go if you are holding it in your heart. I am a worshipper, and so daily, I'm crying out, "God remove the blockage!" I don't want to block true worship from flowing. If I don't cry out to God constantly, I could prevent the people from experiencing a genuine move of God in worship, and I will get no results in the Spirit.

What are the benefits of pure worship from a clean heart? It's God's manifested glory released so that the people are blessed. Signs and wonders will flow to worshippers. We saw that in Acts 5 on the previous morning. Being on one accord was the key to releasing healing through the apostles. They had no blockage in their hearts. This is what God is ready to see in the churches. A praise team up singing and worshipping on one accord so that the glory is released to heal and set free the captives. A preacher standing before the people with a heart clean and pure, preaching under the glory of God and not a gift. This preaching from a heart that has no blockage will extend to the people's sound doctrine, a word that's straight from God to break the chains off the people. It cannot be a word preached from a heart that is fussing, criticizing, blasting, or bragging in the sight of the people, which will bring no glory to God. Is this why few souls come to church and are saved? Listen, there is a whole lot of preaching and singing going on, but from hearts with blockages!

What's blocking your flow? What's blocking your blessing? It's high time to lie down and allow the ultimate surgeon to do supernatural surgery on your heart. God will remove the blockage so He can flow through you and change your life forever. In doing so, the lives of the people who come into contact with you will be changed as well. No more blockage in the heart, which causes poor worship! Give your heart and will to the Father. Then love Him with your whole heart, with all of your soul, and with all of your mind! This is the first step in removing blockage. Love your enemies, bless those who curse you, do good to those who hate you, and pray for those who falsely accuse you. These are more steps instructing us on how to remove the blockage.

DAY 12 MEMORY SCRIPTURES AND NOTES

Genesis 6:5 - *Then the Lord saw that the wickedness of man was great in the earth, and that every intent of the thoughts of his heart was only evil continually.*

Mark 12:30-31 - *And you shall love the Lord your God with all your heart, with all your soul, with all your mind, and with all your strength.' This is the first commandment. And the second, like it, is this: 'You shall love your neighbor as yourself.' There is no other commandment greater than these."*

Matthew 5:44 - *But I say to you, love your enemies, bless those who curse you, do good to those who hate you, and pray for those who spitefully use you and persecute you,*

DAY 13
WORSHIP THAT MATTERS

It is imperative that the heart is in the correct alignment for true worship to flow. It really is a matter of the heart's condition when it comes to true, authentic worship. God is asking what is the matter with the heart. He's not pleased with the so-called worship that's being released in the church. We have the sign outside *Worship Service*, but the heart does not correspond with the worship.

There is a sound that flows from the heart that is not in compliance with God's Word. Proverbs 4:23 says, "Out of the heart flows the issues of life." The issues flowing out of our hearts are contaminating our worship. Let us use some examples... A sister is having an affair with someone's husband within the church now. She is on the praise team with the man's wife and attempts to usher the congregation into the presence of God through her worship songs. Do we call this pure worship? Absolutely not! Unfortunately, this is really happening; it is a valid scenario. I had to get on the phone with a woman and her husband in a situation like this and pray for healing and restoration.

The Heart of Worship

Another example is a pastor holding unforgiveness in his heart against his wife for whatever reason, standing in the pulpit to worship and preach. Will his worship be pure? Absolutely not! These are some of the issues flowing from the heart that cause impure worship.

God is ready to release a glory cloud in the midst of His people but can't because He only responds to true worship that is in Spirit and in truth. It really is a matter of the heart because it carries so many unclear issues. In the previous chapters, we talked about circumcising our hearts because God gets no glory from a church without His Spirit or pure worship. He is looking for a glorious church bringing forth pure worship.

Look at the Scripture Ephesians 5:27. It says nothing verbatim about the heart, but it's clear through the eyes of the Spirit that God is talking about our hearts. He says, "That he might present her to himself a glorious church, not having spot or wrinkle or any such thing, but that she should be holy and with no blemish." God said holy without blemish, and He's not talking about a church building. Yes, God wants a church building that is beautifully organized and clean without any blemishes, but what does it cost to have a beautiful church building full of blemished hearts? Will a glorious worship esteem from the services? No, only vain worship from hearts that are full of vain issues of this life.

Children love one another with pure love, forgiving one another.

2 Corinthians 13:11 says, "Finally, brethren, farewell. Become complete. Be of good comfort, be of one mind, live in peace; and the God of love and peace will be with you." Fellowshipping together in love is God's plan; fellowship from a pure heart worshipping in the beauty of holiness is the Father's will. Why so much strife in the body of Christ? It's because of the matter of our hearts. "By this, all will know that you are My disciples, if you have love for one another." (John 13: 35, NKJV)

When we begin to really fellowship with God and one another, we will begin to encounter worship like we have never in our lives. The heart is what God is after, for it's the matter of our hearts. Worship is a matter of our hearts.

The Heart of Worship

DAY 13 MEMORY SCRIPTURES AND NOTES

Ephesians 5:27 - *That He might present her to Himself a glorious church, not having spot or wrinkle or any such thing, but that she should be holy and without blemish.*

John 13:35 - *By this, all will know that you are My disciples, if you have love for one another.*

_____

_____

_____

_____

_____

_____

_____

_____

_____

_____

_____

_____

_____

DAY 14

THE HEART THAT MATTERS TO GOD

You may ask why the heart matters to God? Our hearts are the beginning of our actions, attitudes, and even our will. When our hearts are in alignment with God's heartbeat, then we will forgive as He forgives, and our actions will show His will in our lives. Saying, "Father, if it is Your will, take this cup away from Me; nevertheless not My will, but Yours, be done." (Luke 22: 42)

The will of the Father is to have a heart to worship Him genuinely. When it comes to worship in song, God is not looking at how good the song sounds, but He's listening for the sound of your heart. What sound is extended from the heart that can get His attention and respond in His presence?

Worship is a lifestyle. If the heart is not circumcised, how will we really express a lifestyle of holiness? The heart matters, and the heart must go through the circumcision process to worship God according to His Word, in Spirit and truth, not our flesh. The flesh is entirely against the Spirit, so it will never worship God. "For the flesh lusts against the Spirit, and the Spirit against the flesh; and these are contrary to one another, so that you do not do the things that you wish." (Galatians 5:17)

The flesh represents the old man, and the old sinful nature will not and cannot worship God. It is the purity of the heart that worships God. This is why we're not getting the results of God's presence in our worship services. The flesh is trying to worship God, and it will never work. We will not encounter a manifestation of God's glory by worshipping out of an impure heart. The heart matters in worship, and the heart matters to God.

Sadly, many think it doesn't matter that God said to come as you are. Yes, God did, but in time, you have to work on your heart. Forgive and love others by loosing yourself from contamination of the heart. Get rid of the toxic things that come into your heart. The heart harbors many issues, and if we don't deal with the issues and just come to worship God, it makes the worship vain.

In these last days, we need as many God encounters and manifestations of His glory in our worship services as we can get. There is so much more God wants to do by pouring out His Spirit, but He's looking into the hearts of the churches' worship. Too often, we begin the service by talking, laughing, and joking. No one is serious about the worship services. The same repetitious prayers are being

The Heart of Worship

prayed as though they're just going through the motions or following the routine order of service.

It's time to wake up out of our sleep and really go to the throne of grace to pray and worship. If the heart did not matter to God, then why would God send a flood to destroy man after He looked at man's heart and saw the wickedness of their actions? It made Him angry, which tells me that the heart matters.

What is true worship without a true heart? What is it to love without honesty and purity of the heart? It starts with the heart. Proverbs 23:7(a) says, "For as he thinks in his heart, so is he." The heart speaks loudly through actions. This is why I can discern true worship. Watch the lifestyle of that individual because those actions speak through worship. Malice, bitterness, and jealousy will speak loudly. Sin speaks loudly, and you can feel it when a worship leader stands before the people to worship and usher you into God's presence. The heart will start speaking. Just watch a person's action, and you will know the matter of their heart. It's not their words, it's their actions. The actions speak louder than the words because the actions are steering the actions that are gleaming from the heart. I love the phrase… "Love is only words until it speaks through the actions." Love is genuine when it is shown forth through actions. The heart will demonstrate love. Worship is a matter of the heart, and the heart matters to God.

DAY 14 MEMORY SCRIPTURES AND NOTES

Luke 22:42 - *Saying, "Father, if it is Your will, take this cup away from Me; nevertheless not My will, but Yours, be done."*

Galatians 5:17 - *For the flesh lusts against the Spirit, and the Spirit against the flesh; and these are contrary to one another, so that you do not do the things that you wish.*

DAY 15

WHAT DOES WORSHIP MEAN TO YOU?

As I sit here and meditate, I think about what worship really means to the people of God. We know worship is a lifestyle, but here, I am referring to worship in songs. As worship leaders, we must ask ourselves if we are genuinely worshipping God when we stand before the people at our services. Examine your hearts.

I am a worship leader, and I understand that worship is more than a song. It's the posture of my heart. Therefore, daily, I examine my heart. I don't only do it on Sunday morning or before a worship service. This is something I do daily. Paul said, "I die daily." (1 Corinthians 15:31)

Crucifying the flesh is necessary. We give up our will so that the Father has His will in our lives. A surrendered worship leader can open the portals of heaven because God responds to a surrendered and broken heart. Romans 6:6 says, "Knowing this, that our old man has been crucified with Him." Our will has been crucified with Christ. The old self, the old you, no longer lives when you surrender all to Jesus. Therefore, when we stand before people, they don't see us. The people don't recognize us, but they see the glory of God

The Heart of Worship

resting on us. How did John know who Jesus was? John saw the dove resting upon Jesus. The abiding presence of God will rest on us. The Bible says in John 1:32, "I saw the Spirit descending from heaven like a dove, and it remained on Him." John saw the glory resting on Jesus. This glory was descending from heaven above. Now, if the Son of God walked the earth representing the Spirit of God, who are we?

We must do likewise. This is the place where God is drawing His people. Drawing us into His presence in such a way people will look at a worship leader and know they have been in the presence of God. This witness will be the evidence of a circumcised heart and surrendered life.

The glory of God overlooks our hearts in such a way that those around us will be affected by God's presence. When we begin to see this glory resting on God's people, it is evident that they chose to die to themselves, to their flesh. They paid a price to carry this presence with a surrendered heart unto the Father. It's a heart broken in His presence, open so that the Father can pour into it.

This is the end time that we're in. God is seeking for willing hearts. When God sees a willing heart, He will use it for His glory. Look at Isaiah 1:19. "If ye be willing and obedient, ye shall eat the good of the land." So many think of only money and wealth when they read this Scripture. The good is having God's presence with you in the land. Be willing to surrender your energy to the Father. He promised that you would eat well. Every day, your needs will be supplied out of overflow in your life. It starts with the presence dwelling with you and in you. Be willing to worship Jesus with everything within you. I pray that worship leaders with willing hearts will be raised up to worship in truth and shake this nation. When the world looks at us, it will be shaken because they don't just hear a song, but they see God!

DAY 15 MEMORY SCRIPTURES AND NOTES

1 Corinthians 15:31 - *I affirm, by the boasting in you which I have in Christ Jesus our Lord, I die daily.*

Isaiah 1:19 - *If you are willing and obedient, You shall eat the good of the land;*

_____

_____

_____

The Heart of Worship

DAY 16
MAN'S HEART

What is in man's heart? That's the question of the hour. If you analyze man's actions, you will know what's in man's heart. This is why we must guard our hearts. Mark 7:14-23 reveals many evil things that come from the heart. Jesus stated, "It's not what enters a man that defiles him; it's what comes out of a man that defiles a man." *And He said, "What comes out of a man that defiles a man. For from within, out of the heart of men, proceed evil thoughts, adulteries, fornications, murders, 22 thefts, covetousness, wickedness, deceit, lewdness, an evil eye, blasphemy, pride, foolishness. All these evil things come from within and defile a man."* (Mark 17:20-23)

When you see a person who hates someone for absolutely no reason, it's coming from out of evil thoughts in his mind. Those thoughts will become actions or deeds. A man and woman commit adultery, and the root of the matter is what's in the heart. This man's heart deceived him with lust and pride. He acted out the feelings from his heart. You don't commit adultery if you love your spouse. When you're in love, you guard over your relationship. It's the same in the spirit. Your worship of love to the seper should be guarded over. You protect your heart. We must not commit adultery with another. If we do, it causes our worship to be vain.

We must love God with all our hearts. If we do not, all these actions from Mark 7 will extend out from our hearts. If our hearts are defiled, then our worship is defiled. Out of this evil-filled worship, no manifestation of God's presence shall be revealed. What is in your heart will determine whether your worship is genuine or pure. Evil thoughts proceed from a contaminated heart. When we have evil thoughts about someone, whether we have a reason or not, there is something in the heart towards that person that causes us to have evil thoughts. This is what makes our worship impure.

As simple as this seems to be, it is disturbing. It's hurtful to know that our hearts are what separate us from God. We have a choice to evaluate and purify our hearts. When we have an evil eye or thoughts toward someone, that is a result of a corrupted heart. I shared this story a few times about a sister in Christ. Yes, I said a sister in Jesus Christ. This sister one day confessed to me that for a few years, she didn't like me for any specific reason. She went on to say that when you came to the church, I said, "Look at her; she thinks she's cute."

She said she didn't know me but knew my mom. She openly confessed that I had never offended her. She plainly said for no reason she didn't like me. She asked me to forgive her for it, and I told her, "Of course, I forgive you."

You see, those thoughts towards me were from her heart. Her evil eye towards me was her heart speaking aloud. The Bible says to confess our faults to one another, and she did right to get it out. God brought healing, and I was okay because I had no idea she didn't like me. Today, she comes to me for prayer or any spiritual guidance because God circumcised her heart. This is what God intends to do for His children, to clean and purify our hearts so that our worship is pure!

DAY 16 MEMORY SCRIPTURE AND NOTES

Mark 7:14-23 - *When He had called all the multitude to Himself, He said to them, "Hear Me, everyone, and understand: There is nothing that enters a man from outside which can defile him; but the things which come out of him, those are the things that defile a man. If anyone has ears to hear, let him hear!" When He had entered a house away from the crowd, His disciples asked Him concerning the parable. So He said to them, "Are you thus without understanding also? Do you not perceive that whatever enters a man from outside cannot defile him, because it does not enter his heart but his stomach, and is eliminated, thus purifying all foods?" And He said, "What comes out of a man, that defiles a man. For from within, out of the heart of men, proceed evil thoughts, adulteries, fornications, murders, thefts, covetousness, wickedness, deceit, lewdness, an evil eye, blasphemy, pride, foolishness. All these evil things come from within and defile a man."*

DAY 17

A TRUE WORSHIPPER'S HEART

When I shared my message about the posture of the heart with my spiritual daughter, Evangelist Renee Strong, she shared these thoughts with me:

"When I think of doubt and the posture of a true worshipper's heart, some things come to mind. Doubt in the heart is one being a heart that is conditioned to the things of the world, which I call "conditional spirituality." However, a true worshipper's heart is surrendered in submission to the sovereignty of God with thanksgiving and gratitude, just as the sovereign God did empty Himself, empowered and poured into His Son, Jesus Christ so that the world go to the cross and receive His blood for the remissions of sins. A true worshipper's heart is unlike physical worship, where the posture may be visible to others; however, its posture is first evidenced to others by the outpour of the fruit of the Spirit.

The posture of a worshipper's heart is a spiritual condition that starts within and flows outwardly. The Bible tells us that we ought to guard our hearts, for out of it springs the issues of life. Therefore, if we are careful stewards of our hearts, the issues of life will not be a hindrance to our worship of God. The posture of a true worshipper's heart is likened to a deer that pants by the river brook, hungering and thirsting for a relationship with God. Finally, I compare the posture of a true worshipper's heart to "the rising of the sun, in the presence of God, and giving way to the lesser light in humility of the Creator, God." ~ Evangelist Renee Strong

Thank you, Evangelist Strong, for your spiritual insight into the true worshipper's heart.

DAY 17 MEMORY SCRIPTURES AND NOTES

Proverbs 4:23 - *Keep your heart with all diligence, For out of it spring the issues of life.*

Psalms 42:1 - *As the deer pants for the water brooks, So pants my soul for You, O God.*

The Heart of Worship

DAY 18

EXCERPT FROM "WORSHIP AT THE WELL"

It came even to pass, as the trumpeters and singers were as one, to make one sound to be heard in praising and thanking the LORD; and when they lifted up their voice with the trumpets and cymbals and instruments of musick, and praised the LORD, saying, For he is good; for his mercy endureth for ever: that then the house was filled with a cloud, even the house of the LORD; So that the priests could not stand to minister by reason of the cloud: for the glory of the LORD had filled the house of God (2 Chronicles 5:13-14).

The singers were on one accord; they were as one. They made a sound in harmony and were in agreement. When our spirits agree with the Spirit of God, it brings in a supernatural sound. This is the sound we need from a praise team, choir, and our churches. Here in this Scripture, there is a demonstration of oneness and the power of awareness. Out of it was the glory of God manifested in the presence of the people. They began to sing or say, "He is good, for His mercy endureth forever." One person wasn't saying, "God isn't good to me or complaining about something." Everyone sang the same thing, and this ushered in God's response, which was the release of His glory! God saw the agreement; it got His attention.

Matthew 18:20 says, "Where two or three are gathered together in my name, there will I be in the midst of them." God came in and moved miraculously because He saw the oneness. This is the glory He's ready to release in the churches. There is too much competitiveness and division in the house of God. And until we kill the flesh and circumcise our hearts, we will not encounter the latter glory.

Worship is when you lay down your will, kill your flesh, and yield *your* spirit to agree with the Spirit of God. Supernatural power is revealed. Come and get on one accord with the Holy Spirit, and watch God move in your life like never. Worship is our key to everything! Yes, if we had a lifestyle of worship, we would have a fulfilled life. Bring yourself in agreement with our heavenly Father and encounter the supernatural over and over again, for there is a power in agreement!

Praise Team Leaders, please get the revelation from this Scripture; it was not the person singing the song. It was the agreement with God that He was good. On your praise team, if everyone is on one accord and in agreement with God, the glory shall be released!

DAY 18 MEMORY SCRIPTURES AND NOTES

Matthew 8:15-20 – *"Moreover if your brother sins against you, go and tell him his fault between you and him alone. If he hears you, you have gained your brother. But if he will not hear, take with you one or two more, that 'by the mouth of two or three witnesses every word may be established.' And if he refuses to hear them, tell it to the church. But if he refuses even to hear the church, let him be to you like a* heathen and a tax collector. *"Assuredly, I say to you, whatever you bind on earth will be bound in heaven, and whatever you loose on earth will be loosed in heaven. "Again I say to you that if two of you agree on earth concerning anything that they ask, it will be done for them by My Father in heaven. For where two or three are gathered together in My name, I am there in the midst of them."*

_____

_____

_____

_____

The Heart of Worship

DAY 19
THE NATURAL CIRCUMCISION

Let's close this book with more detailed, biblical information about circumcision. When we think about circumcision, we instantly think of pain. Circumcision is a ritual operation that removes all or part of the foreskin from the male sex organ. It functions in most cultures as a right of passage or an initiation ceremony into adulthood.

And God said to Abraham: "As for you, you shall keep My covenant, you and your descendants after you throughout their generations. 10 This is My covenant which you shall keep, between Me and you and your descendants after you: Every male child among you shall be circumcised; 11 and you shall be circumcised in the flesh of your foreskins, and it shall be a sign of the covenant between Me and you. (Genesis 17:9-11)

This was God's covenant required in the natural, but God also requires a circumcision of the heart in the spiritual realm. He commands us to cut off the foreskin of our hearts. This natural circumcision is symbolic of spiritual circumcision because of the cutting away. Although circumcision was required by the mosaic law, the right was

The Heart of Worship

neglected during the dark days when the people of Israel wandered into the wilderness. This was an act of disobedience.

God is requiring us to circumcise the heart. Cut off the malice, backbiting, hatred, jealousy, strife, rebellion, and every corruption of the heart. When we wander into life and ignore the circumstances of our hearts, this is disobedience. Joshua came and resumed the ritual covenant with the generations born in the wilderness. Joshua 5: 2-3 says, "At that time the LORD said unto Joshua, Make thee sharp knives, and circumcise again the children of Israel the second time. And Joshua made him sharp knives, and circumcised the children of Israel at the hill of the foreskins." Per God's instructions, Joshua circumcised the generation that was born in the wilderness. They all stayed in their place until they were healed. The reason Joshua circumcised the people was so that they could inherit the land flowing with milk and honey. This is the same as in the Spirit. The circumcision of the heart is necessary so we, as the children of God, can inherit all of God's goodness and all of God's promises. An uncircumcised heart hinders us from entering into the secret place where God and all of His goodness reside.

DAY 19 MEMORY SCRIPTURES AND NOTES

Joshua 5:4-8 - *"Now this is why he did so: All those who came out of Egypt—all the men of military age—died in the wilderness on the way after leaving Egypt. All the people that came out had been circumcised, but all the people born in the wilderness during the journey from Egypt had not. The Israelites had moved about in the wilderness forty years until all the men who were of military age when they left Egypt had died, since they had not obeyed the Lord. For the Lord had sworn to them that they would not see the land he had solemnly promised their ancestors to give us, a land flowing with milk and honey. So he raised up their sons in their place, and these were the ones Joshua circumcised. They were still uncircumcised because they had not been circumcised on the way. And after the whole nation had been circumcised, they remained where they were in camp until they were healed."*

_____

_____

_____

_____

_____

_____

_____

_____

The Heart of Worship

DAY 20

CIRCUMCISION OF THE HEART

Uncircumcised hearts separate us from experiencing genuine worship. The heart must be pure to encounter a divine atmosphere of true worship. Moses and the prophets used the term "circumcision" as a symbol for purifying the heart and readiness to hear and obey God. The Lord used Moses to call the people to submit to a circumcision of the heart in the natural realm and repent. God has many Moses in the land, compelling the people to repent and circumcise their hearts so we can have authentic worship. This is absolutely a must if we are to encounter and experience the supernatural of God.

'But if they confess their iniquity and the iniquity of their fathers, with their unfaithfulness in which they were unfaithful to Me, and that they also have walked contrary to Me, and that I also have walked contrary to them and have brought them into the land of their enemies; if their uncircumcised hearts are humbled, and they accept their guilt— then I will remember My covenant with Jacob, and My covenant with Isaac and My covenant with Abraham I

will remember; I will remember the land. (Leviticus 26:40-42)

God made a promise to remember and honor all of His promises if the people would just humble themselves and circumcise their hearts. It's painful, but we must be subject to the will of the Father. We cannot continue with an uncircumcised heart, for if we do, then this is rebellion. A rebellious heart will never genuinely worship the Lord.

Jeremiah 6:10 says, 'To whom shall I speak and give warning, That they may hear? Indeed, their ear is uncircumcised, And they cannot give heed. Behold, the word of the Lord is a reproach to them; They have no delight in it." Here, God even called the generation's ears uncircumcised, meaning that they would rebel against the true doctrine of the Word of God. They would close their ears to the voice of God. That is simply disobedience. Sad, but this is where our own nation is today. The world is full of uncircumcised people refusing to submit, confess, or repent. They refuse to glorify and worship Jesus, the Son of the living God. Instead, this world would perform vain worship from an uncircumcised heart.

In this state of mind and the heart, how will we even encounter God supernaturally? There's no way. This is a clarion call to circumcise our hearts, repent, and come back to the Garden of Eden and genuinely worship the Father in the name of Jesus!

DAY 20 MEMORY SCRIPTURES AND NOTES

Leviticus 26:40-42 - *'But if they confess their iniquity and the iniquity of their fathers, with their unfaithfulness in which they were unfaithful to Me, and that they also have walked contrary to Me, and that I also have walked contrary to them and have brought them into the land of their enemies; if their uncircumcised hearts are humbled, and they accept their guilt— then I will remember My covenant with Jacob, and My covenant with Isaac and My covenant with Abraham I will remember; I will remember the land.*

Jeremiah 6:10 - *'To whom shall I speak and give warning, That they may hear? Indeed their ear is uncircumcised, And they cannot give heed. Behold, the word of the Lord is a reproach to them;They have no delight in it."*

_____

_____

_____

_____

The Heart of Worship

DAY 21

THERE IS SO MUCH MORE!

I will end the book with a recap of the Introduction. Worship is more than a song. It's the love in your heart for the Father. If your worship is just a song, then your worship is in vain. What's the matter with your heart? That's a question to ask ourselves… "What's wrong in my heart? Is my heart truly after the Father? Is my heart really in love with Jesus? Is my heart in tune with the heartbeat of God? What is the matter with my heart?"

When our worship is pure, it flows the love of God. Jesus said if you love Me, You will keep my commandments. This is true worship. When your heart is in love with the Father, it's definitely much more than a song. If the song doesn't reflect your heart, then it's not genuine worship. The key to worship is love. This heart of love unlocks the portals of Heaven, and God responds to that sweet-smelling aroma flowing into His nostrils.

It all starts with a genuine love for God. "By this, we know that we love the children of God when we love God and keep His commandments. For this is the love of God, that we keep His commandments…" (1 John 5: 2-3) God is love so our worship must start with love. Again, I ask, what is the matter with your heart? The matter should be I'm in love

The Heart of Worship

with Jesus. When you've fallen totally in love with the Father, your worship will always be more than a song. Your worship will be the matter of your heart, which is love. God is love, and whoever lives in love with God lives in God. This love will teach you the value of worship. This love will be expressed through any song you sing in worship.

This true love of worship will spring up from the heart to the Father, and in return, God responds to the worship with the manifestation of His presence. His glory is revealed out of genuine worship. Worship Leader, if you ever stand before the people, worshipping in song and the glory doesn't fall, it is because God only responds to hearts of love. Remember, it's from glory to glory in these last days, expressing your heart in worship. Seek God's face diligently and allow Him to fill you with so much love that you are ready to return it back to Him through your worship.

Beloved, it's more than a song. It's a circumcised heart surrendered to the Father! He said in His Word, "I'm seeking that true worshipper." But, will He find you? If yes, let Him find you worshiping in Spirit and in truth (St. John 4: 23-24). My worship is authentic, and it's more than just a song. It's my heartbeat toward the Father!

DAY 21 MEMORY SCRIPTURES AND NOTES

1 John 5:2-4 – *"By this we know that we love the children of God, when we love God, and keep his commandments. For this is the love of God, that we keep his commandments: and his commandments are not grievous. For whatsoever is born of God overcometh the world: and this is the victory that overcometh the world, even our faith."*

St John 4:23-24 – *"But the hour cometh, and now is, when the true worshippers shall worship the Father in spirit and in truth: for the Father seeketh such to worship him. God is a Spirit: and they that worship him must worship him in spirit and in truth."*

KEYS TO BECOMING A WORSHIPPER

1. Salvation - Confess your faults and sins unto God. Confess and believe who God is and receive Him in your heart.

2. Build a relationship with God by studying His Word and meditating on it.

3. Build a prayer life with God. Set time aside every morning. The amount of time initially is not as significant; time will increase as you grow.

4. Guard your relationship with God by decreasing your circle between unhealthy friends or relationships and increasing your time with God.

5. Take time to fast and pray. If there is an issue you're battling with, give it to God. Then, confess the issue and fast and pray.

6. Take time to rest in His presence. Sometimes God just went want you there. Prayer is talking to God and taking time for God to talk to you.

The Heart of Worship

SEVEN DAYS OF FASTING AND PRAYER
~*To Usher You into God's Presence*~

Day One

What is Fasting?

Fasting – the biblical term for going without food. The noun translated as "fast" or "a fasting" is in Hebrew and Nigeria in Greek. It means voluntary abstinence from food. So, the literal Hebrew translation would be "not to eat."

This morning, as you rise, take time to pray and meditate before God. Then, ask His guidance on how you should fast according to your workplace or business. Everyone is different, so I always direct people to ask God to lead and guide them mainly on how to fast. It is between you and God!

Matthew 6:16 – 18. *Moreover, when ye fast, be not, as the hypocrites, of a sad countenance; for they disfigure their faces that they may appear unto men to fast. Verily I say unto you, they have their reward. But thou, when thou fastest, anoint thine head, and wash their face; that thou appear not unto men to fast, but unto thy Father which is in secret: and thy Father, which seeth in secret, shall reward thee openly.*

The Heart of Worship

Notes for Day One

Write down your first-day experience and what you expect to see spiritually within your seven-day journey of fasting and praying.

_____

_____

_____

_____

_____

_____

_____

_____

_____

_____

_____

_____

_____

_____

_____

Day Two

Fasting and Praying

Mark 9:29. *And he said unto them, this kind can come forth by nothing, but by prayer and fasting.*

In the book of Mark, a person with a child foaming from the mouth possessed with a dumb spirit brought his child to the disciples to cast the spirit from the child. But he said the disciples could not cast the demon out. Jesus said, "O faithless generation, how long shall I be with you? How long shall I suffer you? Bring him unto me (Mark 9:19). Jesus was saying to His disciples, "Haven't you learned anything" Don't you know by now that this kind of spirit requires you to be in prayer and fasting?"

This generation does not believe it will take fasting and a lifestyle of prayer for what we are facing in the last days. Satan cannot cast out Satan. These spirits are not coming out if you indulge in sinful activities and do not consecrate yourself before God. No longer can we go through the motions of church antics. From the passage of Scripture, we can gather that the disciples did not equip themselves. Jesus fed them and gave them good instructions and teachings, but did they take heed? Evidently not! Or they could have cast out the spirit from the child. Therefore, we must fast and pray.

Notes for Day Two

Take notes today from the Scriptures provided for Day Two. Write down some experiences you have faced and knew you were not equipped to pray for someone else. Then, take this lesson and decide you will heed God's Word.

Day Three

Declare a Fast Ordained by God

Esther 4:16. *Go, gather together all the Jews that are present in Shushan, and fast ye for me, and neither eat nor drink three days night or day; I also and my maidens will fast likewise; and so, will I go in unto the King, which is not according to the law: and if I perish, I perish.*

We have Esther declaring a fast amongst the people to save her entire generation. Mordecai got word to Esther that Haman, Mordecai's enemy, had plotted to have all the Jews destroyed. This was an enemy against the Jews, and Esther knew the only way to destroy this devil was by fasting and praying. Remember, the Bible says these kinds come out only by fasting and prayer. Esther knew this would be a significant risk, but she was wise; she told Mordecai to gather all the Jews in Shushan and fast for her, to neither eat nor drink for three days and nights. She knew she needed some people standing in the gap before she went before the king. Esther risked her life for a generation. In those days, you would be killed if you went before the king without an invitation. Yet, Esther declared, "If I perish, let me perish!" So she went, and God showed her favor and saved a whole generation because she declared a fast. Will you declare a fast for your family and save a generation?

Notes for Day Three

Today, write down your family members and other families you know who are under attack from the enemy. Then, bring some praying family members together and declare a fast on behalf of your family.

_____

_____

_____

_____

_____

_____

_____

_____

_____

_____

Day Four

Great Will Be Your Reward!

Matthew 6:18. *That thou appear not unto men to fast, but unto thy Father which is in secret; and thy Father, which seeth in secret, shall reward thee openly.*

When you gather the family members you listed on Day Three's Notes to fast, do not announce or discuss this with others. Our fast should be unto God. Gather a few praying partners who will pray secretly, be sincere, and not gossip. It is time to get serious with our praying and fasting.

I have never seen so many Christians and preachers with no prayer life. Jesus prayed to the Father, so it is foolish to think we do not need a prayer life. Some say it does not take all this, but it really does! The world is filled with chaos and confusion. Families going through the churches face wicked principalities and wickedness in high places. There is no doubt in my mind and heart that we all need prayer. No one is exempt, from the poorest to the wealthiest person; we all need it. Fasting and praying is not something you broadcast, but God will reward us openly when we fast and pray in secret. Let us look at Moses' example of how God rewarded him openly before the children of Israel in Exodus 33-34. Moses spent time in God's presence, and the glory

The Heart of Worship

was shining on him publicly? When you fast and pray, people will see the glory in your life and see God moving openly on your circumstances. Just fast and pray; be quiet and let God do the talking by rewarding you openly.

Notes for Day Four

List the things you want God to do personally for you that you have not discussed with anyone. Let this day be very intimate and sacred between you and God. Write down your secrets and confessions to God. He will reward you openly!

_____

_____

_____

_____

_____

_____

_____

_____

Day Five

Ordained by God or Man?

Acts 14:23. *And when they had ordained them elders in every church, and had prayed with fasting, they commended him to the Lord on whom they believed.*

    This Scripture is mainly for pastors and bishops, who ordain ministers for the ministry's work. Pastors must fast and pray before ordaining people. The Bible says to not lay hands suddenly on no man. Why are we so quick to send people out unequipped? I believe one reason is we are building membership this way. I am skeptical when I attend service at a small church; out of 25 members, 15 are ministers. Everyone has not been chosen by God. Leaders need to lay before God and consult Him before ordaining ministers and taking matters into their own hands. People are making a mess out here because they have been ordained by man, not God. God is not pleased with these actions. I see people getting ordained who are committing adultery or fornication. Their character is far from the title they hold in the church. Therefore, God is calling us to fast and pray to receive the needed direction and instructions in our lives. I would rather sit in the back of the church until I learn the truth than be pulled up to receive a title, knowing I am not in the proper standards with God.

The Heart of Worship

Leaders, please fast and pray before ordaining and handing out titles!

Notes for Day Five

If you are a pastor, write down some mistakes in ordaining or placing people in positions without fasting and praying. Be honest with yourself and God; then ask Him if this is one of the reasons your church is not growing. If you are not, write down when you knew you were not in the proper standards with God and took on a title/position unworthily. What did you learn or will do differently now?

_____

_____

_____

_____

_____

_____

_____

_____

Day Six

Choose the Fast of God

Isaiah 58:6. *Is not this the fast that I have chosen? To loose the bands of wickedness, to undo the heavy burdens, and to let the oppressed go free, and that ye break every yoke?*

God was letting us know He must call the fast to be effective and ordained by Him. Many fasts we are doing are of man, and we see no results. If God did not call it, then you might as well EAT! God said in the Scriptures, we read that His fast breaks every yoke and loose the bands of wickedness. The fast of God breaks every chain in our lives. It will set the captive free and deliver us from lust. But because we are not listening to God and doing our own thing, we are not experiencing deliverance in our churches and homes. We need to ask ourselves whether we are just dieting or fasting. Remember that this is what got Eve and Adam in trouble. Satan tempted them with food, a piece of fruit. Then he tried to tempt Jesus with food while fasting in the wilderness. The devil told Jesus to turn the stone into bread. This is clear evidence that the devil never wants us to fast and pray because even he knows the benefits. He knows that we will tear his dark kingdom down when we get serious about praying and fasting! Check your motive when you fast. Make sure it is the fast to break yokes and loose the bands of wickedness, not for selfish gain.

Notes for Day Six

Today, ask yourself, "Why am I really doing this seven-day fast?" Before you start it, make sure you have the right motive. Name some strongholds you want to be loosed out of your life or family members' lives.

_____

_____

_____

_____

_____

_____

_____

_____

_____

Day Seven

Follow the Example of Jesus

Matthew 26:41. The spirit indeed is willing; but the flesh is weak.

Today, I want you to meditate on the very importance of why you are fasting. I know this is the last day but think about our Savior, Jesus Christ, as you end it. This Scripture reminds us how our spirit is willing to do right, but the flesh is not; therefore, we must fast and pray. Jesus was in the garden of Gethsemane, and He asked the disciples to pray for Him. But when He returned from praying, they were asleep. They were willing to pray with Jesus for one hour, but their flesh could not withstand it because of its weakness. Therefore, the flesh must come under the subjection of the Spirit of the Lord. Fasting and prayer bring the flesh under the authority of the Spirit of God!

Remember, Jesus fasted 40 days and 40 nights; afterward, the devil tempted Him. Jesus overcame the temptations of Satan through fasting and prayer, so we must do the same. If you are a Christian and you are not taking the time to fast and pray, I can assure you that many decisions you make will be from your emotions and intellect, not your spirit. Allow God to lead you as you fast and pray, but He cannot lead you if you refuse to submit to His will. You will learn to submit to God's will as you learn how to fast and pray. If Jesus did, who are we to say that we cannot?

Notes for Day Seven

Write down notes on your temptation experiences. Then, name some victories in your life that you know you have overcome because of fasting and prayer.

_____

_____

_____

_____

_____

_____

_____

_____

_____

_____

The Heart of Worship

The Heart of Worship

MY PRAYER FOR YOU!

Today, I pray that you rise up from the place you're in and step into the deeper place God has for you. Know that greater is He that is in you than he that is in the world. Open your heart and receive all God's goodness for your life. He has begun a good work in you, so push forward into it. In Jesus' name, may He break off every burden from your shoulders. So, you can run and not be weary, walk, and not faint. Fly higher into the reckoning of the Spirit.

You are more than a conqueror in Jesus Christ. I pray you to be encouraged. Be strong and courageous, and don't be afraid or dismayed, for the Lord is with you. Break further in the new season in Jesus' name.

God, cover Your child and build them up in the faith. I pray the Lord bless you and keep you. The Lord makes His face to shine upon you; the Lord lifts His countenance upon you and gives you peace in Jesus' name.

May God circumcise your heart so nothing will separate you from His presence. Amen!

Prophetess Latina Teele

"My Heart of Love and Worship"

The "Expression of our Hearts" is expressing the love of the Father through the demonstration of our hearts. Worship is the expression of the love we have for the Father. But the love is not completed until we love one another as well. I love my Heavenly Father, but my love is proven when I love my sisters and brothers, or else I am a liar.

"If someone says, "I love God," and hates his brother, he is a liar; for he who does not love his brother whom he has seen, [a]how can he love God whom he has not seen?" (1 John 4:20) We have this commandment from Him. Whoever loves God must also love his brother! Therefore, worship is the expression of our love for God, but we can't love God and hate one another, or else our worship is vain.

What is the condition of your heart? What condition are our hearts in? Is the condition unforgiveness, hatred, resentment, jealousy, envy, pride, lust, strife, or is the condition love, peace, joy, temperance? *I, the Lord, search the heart, I try the reins, even to give every man according to his ways, According to the fruit of his doings.* (Jeremiah 17:10) Leaders are not exempt from this principle!

God asks again. *"What Is The Condition of Your Heart?"* Examine your heart and discuss your condition privately with the Lord. He already knows.

The Heart: Jeremiah 17:9 declares, "The heart is deceitful above all things, and desperately wicked: who can know it?" When we look around this world and see all the wickedness, it proves that it's a heart thing. Hurt, betrayal, rejection, manipulation, strife, you name it! It is all a result of the heart. As I read Genesis 6:5-7 daily, I grieve and weep sometimes. Just to imagine God saw so much wickedness in the heart of man, He regretted He had made man.

God said, "I will wipe out the human race from the earth."

Thank You, Father, for having mercy on us! Love with everything within you, and love the Lord unconditionally. I used to say that if I'm going to serve the devil, I'm going to serve him real good and not half-heartily. If you're going to serve Jesus, serve Him good! Give Him your all, not in between. Just like in a marriage, you don't want to share your spouse. God is a jealous God, and He knows when we share our hearts. Give Him your whole heart. I think it's foolish to play with an all-powerful God. Be serious about your relationship. Seek Him diligently, and He shall be found. Because of what's unfolding on this earth, you have to get more closer to Jesus. Walk, talk, live, worship, and love Him daily with your whole heart. This is my heart of love and worship!

About The Author

Prophetess Latina Teele is an author, teacher, entrepreneur, and recording artist. Her passion for her Savior, Jesus Christ, is heard, felt, and known through her melodious voice and songs of worship and inspiration.

She is a powerful evangelist who travels extensively around the world, preaching and teaching the Word of God with charisma and anointing. Her insight into the Word of God and the spiritual discipline of worship are both transforming and life-changing! As a result, she is a much sought-after speaker of this century.

For More Information...

Email: latinateele@gmail.com

Website: www.breakingfreencministries.com

Made in the USA
Middletown, DE
09 February 2025